The Adventures of Pickle

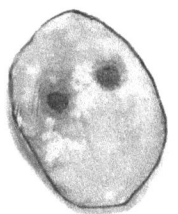

Zelda Mothins

Illustrations by Hattie Hyder

Copyright © 2021 Zelda Mothins

This edition 2023

All rights reserved, including the right to reproduce this book, or portions thereof in any form. No part of this text may be reproduced, transmitted, downloaded, decompiled, reverse engineered, or stored, in any form or introduced into any information storage and retrieval system, in any form or by any means, whether electronic or mechanical without the express written permission of the author.

This is a work of fiction. Names and characters are the product of the author's imagination and any resemblance to actual persons, living or dead, is entirely coincidental.

The views expressed in this work are solely those of the author and do not necessarily reflect the views of the publisher, and the publisher hereby disclaims any responsibility for them.

ISBN: 978-1-915889-65-2

PublishNation
www.publishnation.co.uk

The Adventures of Pickle

Pickle was a pebble.

But he was no ordinary pebble.

For one, he had a name — a proper name.

He wasn't some random pebble on the beach. He was special, with an important job to do. But he didn't know that straight away.

Pickle thought back to when he first realised he was different. He was sitting on the beach, minding his own business, when all of a sudden a small hand reached down and swiftly picked him up. He felt a bit sick from the motion.

He had been picked up before, but had always been instantly tossed out into the water. He hated that. It always took so much time to be washed back up onto the shore again.

But this time was different. This hand was soft, ever so gently tickling him as the little girl turned him over and over in her hand, gazing at him with wide open eyes.

"Mummy, Mummy, I found the ONE!" she shouted.

She was a bit loud and Pickle felt a little frightened.

He felt her gaze upon him again, then all of a sudden there was darkness.

Where was he now?

The small hand touched him once more and squeezed him tight.

He felt cocooned and warm and somehow instinctively knew that everything was going to be alright.

Pickle's New Job

Pickle woke with a jolt. He felt a bit hot as the sun was streaming in through the window.

He looked around. It appeared that he was up high, on some sort of ledge. On closer inspection, he realised he was in a bedroom, perched on a windowsill. The window was open and there was a lovely summer breeze coming in.

Pickle closed his eyes for a second and hoped that, wherever he was, they would treat him better than the previous family. They were mean to him and used him as a ball for their silly dog. But that's another story!

Suddenly, he was swooped up by the small hand and turned over and over. He felt that horrible sicky feeling again.

"I shall call you Pickle," the little girl said and brushed her lips gently against him.

Pickle blushed, as only a pebble can, and a warmth filled him, making him feel safe and happy.

"You actually have eyes," she stated, running her fingers over him and the two small indentations.

Errr, yes, he thought. *How do you think I can see?*

"You have to help me, though," she said seriously. "And protect me from the others."

Pickle thought the little girl sounded worried.

He wondered who the 'others' were and whether they were out to hurt his new friend. He swallowed hard.

"Don't worry though," she said. "We are going to have great fun!" And with that she placed him ever so gently back on the windowsill in the warmth of the sun. He sighed heavily and felt content.

The next morning, Pickle woke to a very loud noise. His heart began beating fast and for a split second he wished he was back on the beach, minding his own business.

Suddenly, there was loud thumping — so loud he thought the whole house might actually explode.

He was scared. He wasn't keen on loud noises.

He heard the little girl stomp into the room, shouting loudly and crying at the same time.

He decided to stay very still, barely breathing.

He heard a man and woman's voice next, but they weren't shouting, thankfully. They sounded calm. *Maybe they're her parents?* he thought.

"How many pebbles do you have now?" the man asked the little girl gently.

Picked remained still. The little girl whispered something, but Pickle could barely hear her.

The man spoke again. "Ten? How can you have ten? You've literally just woken up."

Pickle frowned. Were there more of him? He looked around but couldn't spot anyone. He closed his eyes tightly and tried to block everything out.

After a short while, the little girl stopped crying and it was quiet.

Pickle opened one eye carefully and squinted.

The man and the lady were cuddling the little girl. She seemed much calmer now and he noticed that her face wasn't so red.

"How many pebbles now?" the man asked again.

Pickle wondered if this was some sort of game. If so, he wanted to join in. It sounded fun!

"Just Pickle," the girl said and swooped him up and held him close to her chest. "But Pickle can stay — he's my friend."

Pickle felt a warm glow whoosh over him. He had no idea what was going on, but he knew his mission was somehow to help this little girl.

He sighed and closed his eyes. He was suddenly feeling very tired.

Anxiety

The following morning when Pickle stirred, he was no longer in the bedroom. He seemed to be outside.

He felt a cool breeze brush past him. He looked down and appeared to be moving very fast, so fast, in fact, that he felt a little scared.

Suddenly, the motion stopped and he was inside the little girl's hand again.

"Meet Pickle," the little girl said, and he was passed over to another small hand.

But this hand was different. Not soft at all and it was all dirty, too.

Pickle looked up and met the gaze of a small boy eyeing him curiously.

"Why have you given a pebble a name?" the little boy sneered.

"Why not?" the little girl said.

The boy shrugged, roughly passed Pickle back to the little girl and rode his bike off down the road laughing loudly.

"Don't worry, Pickle. He just doesn't understand. Let's go back inside and have a little chat. We could watch some TV, if you like."

Pickle smiled. He didn't want to see the little boy again. Who was *he* to question Pickle's name? He loved his name. He had never had a name before and it made him feel quite important.

Back up in the safety of the bedroom, the little girl placed Pickle on her lap.

"I need to tell you something," she whispered.

Pickle hoped it wasn't bad news. He was beginning to like it here.

"You are...a pebble!" she exclaimed.

Pickle frowned. He already knew that.

"When I get butterflies in my tummy, it's called anxiety," she said.

Butterflies? Pickle thought. He was confused now, how did the butterflies manage to get in the little girl's tummy?

"Mummy and Daddy say that I have something called 'Autism'. Not just Autism, but PDA, which stands for Pathological Demand Avoidance. Oh, and I also have ADHD, too," she explained with an uncertain smile.

Pickle had no idea what all these words and letters meant, but the little girl seemed happy right now, and that was good enough for him.

He studied her as she stared out of the window, lost in thought, and just wished that he understood more and that everything didn't have to sound so complicated.

Why oh why did I have to be a pebble and not a human? His brain began to hurt, so he turned his thoughts back to the beach and the water to calm himself. That always helped.

"You are going to represent my anxiety," she suddenly blurted out.

Wait, what? he thought. Anxiety? He wasn't sure if he liked the sound of that.

"When I start to feel overwhelmed, I liken my anxiety to pebbles. They build up and up in my tummy until I EXPLODE!" she shouted very loudly. Her face started to turn a bit red.

Pickle was really worried now. He didn't want to be eaten by this little girl. And how could there be room for pebbles and butterflies in her tummy? It was all so confusing!

"Don't worry, though," she said, softly stroking him again. "You are the ONLY pebble who is allowed to stay with me and I need you to help me fight off the others and keep me calm."

Pickle sighed in relief. He could stay? But he had to fight. He wasn't sure he was up for that, but then again, he did like a challenge!

Struggles

"Hurry up or we will be late!" boomed a voice up the stairs.

The little girl angrily threw her shoe across the room with force. Something fell to the ground and smashed.

Uh-oh, thought Pickle.

She hated to be hurried up. Why couldn't she just do things in her own time and own speed. Why was the world always in such a rush?

"Are you coming?" the voice shouted again, this time even louder.

Pickle looked at the little girl. Her face was all squished up like she was going to cry.

She ran out of her bedroom and threw the other shoe angrily down the stairs.

Oh no, thought Pickle. He was pretty sure she shouldn't have done that. He took a deep breath, unsure what to expect next. He wanted to cover his ears, but didn't have any, so he closed his eyes tightly shut instead.

It went quiet. Where was everyone ? He wished he had legs so could run the down the stairs to summon help.

Suddenly, the mummy appeared in the doorway, "Are you okay, Pumpkin?" she asked.

Pickle frowned. *Who was Pumpkin?* He looked round the room but could see no one who was orange and round!

The little girl growled back, hissed at the mummy just like a snake, and suddenly grabbed him roughly.

Pickle tried to remain still, but the little girl was squeezing him so tightly he had to gasp for air.

The mummy crouched down, giving Pickle a chance to study her. She had a kind face and a soft voice. Maybe she would be able to calm the little girl down.

"Shall we put one shoe on up here and the other downstairs?" she asked.

The little girl growled at the mummy, but didn't seem quite so angry. Her face was still red, though.

Pickle wondered if this was the anxiety the little girl had told him about. If so, he didn't like it one bit. It was scary!

He felt her grip on him relax a little and he let out a deep breath.

Within a couple of minutes, the little girl scrambled to her feet, picked up the one remaining shoe and bounced downstairs, still holding Pickle tight. The mummy followed.

Pickle quite liked being bounced up and down. He much preferred that to being on the little girl's bike. He didn't like that sensation at all!

Once downstairs, Pickle was set down on the table whilst the little girl put on her other shoe and did up the laces.

Pickle noticed the mummy and daddy in the kitchen, softly talking to one another.

The mummy looked a bit sad and the daddy whispered something in her ear and put his arm around her shoulders.

Pickle hated seeing anyone upset. He hoped this was going to be a nice place to live as it was a long way back to the beach.

The Little Black Dog

Pickle was enjoying a rest on the table when all of a sudden a huge pink tongue licked his whole being.

He tried to focus, but whatever it was backed away quickly.

"Woof!"

Pickle nearly jumped off the table in fright.

"Woof, woof!"

Oh no, he thought. *Surely they don't have a dog as well?*

He had had his suspicions that there was a four-legged family member, but they hadn't yet been introduced.

He really wasn't keen on dogs, ever since the last family used him as a ball for their dog to fetch at the beach one time. He shuddered at the memory.

The wet, pink tongue covered him again and Pickle squeezed his eyes tight. *Please, please leave me alone*, he prayed.

All of a sudden he was free falling and hit the ground with a thud.

The tongue covered him again and Pickle saw his life flash before his eyes. He didn't want to leave the world this way! He was supposed to help the little girl with her anxiety and butterflies. And the Pumpkin, what about the Pumpkin? He hadn't even met him yet!

Pickle opened one eye slowly and saw a little black dog staring at him with his head cocked to one side.

"Woof!"

Pickle didn't know what to do in return. He couldn't bark back, that was for sure, so he stayed very still and decided to play dead.

The dog nudged him with his wet nose again, wanting to play.

There wasn't much Pickle could do. He was a pebble after all. What did the dog expect?

The dog suddenly started barking loudly and jumped up at the back door.

The mummy and daddy walked in and the little black dog went mad. Pickle had never seen anything like it.

"What's that on the floor?" the mummy asked and pointed to Pickle.

The daddy walked over and picked up Pickle. "Ahh, she left Pickle here. She was going to take him with her to school."

School? Pickle wondered what that meant.

"Maybe she can take him tomorrow instead," the mummy said.

Pickle wasn't sure if he wanted to go to this place called school. What if he didn't like it?

He thought back to this morning and the shoe incident. Was that because the little girl didn't want to go to this school place either? Maybe that was where this thing called anxiety happened?

He would have to do his best to try and find out. He didn't want the little girl throwing any of her shoes at him, that was for sure!

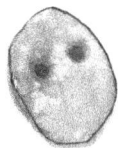

Pickle wondered what time the little girl would be back home. He missed her company and her tickles.

Thankfully, though, he was back on the table and out of reach of the little black dog, although he could still see him sitting in the corner of the room with his tongue hanging out.

Pickle thought back to this morning and wondered if he could have done anything more to help the little girl. But having no arms or legs, let alone a voice, made things very difficult indeed.

After what seemed like an eternity, the mummy and daddy left to collect the little girl from this place called school. He hoped she would be in a good mood when she came back home.

All he could do in the meantime was wait, with the little black dog staring in his direction.

Finally, the back door swung wide open and the little black dog went crazy again.

This was certainly a noisy household, Pickle thought.

"Pickle, there you are! I'm so sorry I left you here," the little girl exclaimed and rushed to pick him up, turning him over and over in her hands.

Pickle felt the sicky feeling rise again.

"Let's go upstairs and I will tell you all about my day."

Once in the little girl's bedroom, she began to talk excitedly about her day. Pickle lay there on her lap, listening intently, trying to understand all the words, but also feeling rather sleepy.

He eventually drifted off, dreaming of what tomorrow might bring. He wondered if it would be another school day and if the anxiety the little girl spoke of happened every day. He would have to be ready to help her if it did.

The Dentist

The next morning, everything seemed calm. Almost too calm.

Pickle was laying in bed, next to the little girl, but he was right on the edge. He dared not move in case he fell out and toppled onto the floor. With no legs, he would certainly be stuck until she woke up.

The little girl suddenly groaned, as if remembering something. Pickle stiffened.

"Oh, Pickle," she said, picking him up and studying him. "I've got to go to the dentist this morning and I really don't want to." She groaned again.

Pickle wondered what on earth the dentist was. Maybe it was something to do with school?

"Have you cleaned your teeth already?" he heard the daddy shout up the stairs.

"Yes!" she shouted back, winking at Pickle.

She got up, quickly dressed, and ran into the bathroom.

Pickle waited patiently.

She ran back into the bedroom within seconds, smiling and saying, "Shhhh. Don't tell them, but I haven't done them. I hate doing them!"

Pickle guessed she was referring to her teeth.

Soon, the whole family were in the car. He was in the back with the little girl and the mummy and daddy were up front.

Music was playing on the stereo, but somehow he could feel a sort of tension in the air. It felt rather heavy. Had the mummy and daddy fallen out? That happened a lot where he lived before.

After a short while, the car stopped and Pickle looked out of the window. They appeared to be in a car park. He remembered the daddy saying now that the dentist lady would come and get them when they were ready — something to do with Covid. He wasn't too sure what Covid meant, but everyone seemed to be talking about it all the time.

He glanced up at the little girl. She had a funny look on her face. He studied the daddy's face in the rearview mirror. He had the same look, too.

The mummy turned around, "Ready then, Pumpkin?" she asked.

Pumpkin? He didn't realise Pumpkin had got in the car, too. Was he playing hide and seek? He certainly couldn't see him anywhere!

Just then the little girl shook her head and snarled, baring her teeth. Pickle didn't know much, but he knew this was a sign for danger. Or did it mean she was ready for someone to look at her teeth now? He was confused.

"Come on, it will be fine," the mummy said in a slightly softer tone.

The little girl shook her head again and kicked the back of the daddy's seat, causing him to jolt forwards towards the steering wheel.

Pickle cringed. He really didn't think that was a good idea.

All of a sudden there was a tap tap at the window and a lady peered in.

The daddy wound down his window. "Hello there," she said. "Are we ready to go in?" She looked at the little girl, who growled under her breath and kicked the seat again, this time much harder.

Pickle was suddenly squeezed extremely tightly and just as he thought he was about to faint, the little girl released her grip, chucked him on the seat next to her, and leaned forward to punch the daddy on his shoulder.

The lady pulled a face, tutted and said, "Come on, you did just fine last time. Let's go in now, shall we, and stop wasting time?"

The little girl suddenly pulled the daddy's hair, hard. The mummy sighed heavily and reached out to touch the daddy's hand.

The little girl swooped Pickle up again. Her palms were all sweaty, he noticed, and her face was red again, too. This was not good, he thought.

Pickle had no idea what was happening, but this other lady was obviously the dentist person, and the little girl didn't seem to like her one bit!

He took a sneaky glance up at the little girl, her face still contorted with anger, worry, and tears. He wished he could just reach out and cuddle her.

"I think we will have to leave it for today," the mummy said, leaning across the daddy to talk through the window.

The lady said something Pickle couldn't make out, nodded and walked back across the car park.

The daddy rolled up the window, whilst rubbing his shoulder. The mummy stroked his hair. Her eyes were very watery, Pickle noticed.

He felt the little girl exhale deeply.

Soon they were driving away from the car park and it seemed everyone was relieved. Even the car engine seemed to sigh deeply.

The daddy took a deep breath in and out, and the mummy whispered, "I wish they would understand PDA. I'm going to have to write a letter to them. This can't happen again."

The daddy nodded, his face also wet with silent tears. "Yes, we will. It seems nobody understands her but us."

Pickle contemplated this comment. He had so much to learn about this family and especially the little girl.

Pickle Goes To School

"You're coming to school today!" the little girl exclaimed.

Pickle felt a bit nervous. He'd never been to a school before, and he was kind of hoping the little girl might leave him at home like last time. But then, he didn't want to fall off the table and face the little black dog and his tickly tongue again, either!

The little girl got dressed, slowly. She seemed to be struggling with her tights. Her face was getting redder and redder until she ripped them off and threw them across the room. She folded her arms and shouted out, "I'm not going to school today!"

Pickle frowned. Surely she could try putting them on again, or even ask for help from the mummy or daddy?

He wished he could help, but it was not possible.

The mummy appeared at the doorway and crouched down.

Pickle could smell her perfume, she smelt like pretty flowers. He closed his eyes. A memory fleetingly crossed his mind, a little hazy, but he had definitely smelt that smell before.

"Shall I help you?" the mummy asked the little girl.

"No," came the reply. "Why do I have to get dressed before breakfast anyway?" the little girl argued.

"Because that is what we always do," the mummy replied.

"Well, I'm not going to school today, so there!"

Pickle thought the mummy was going to argue back, but she obviously thought better of it as she just sighed and made her way back downstairs again.

Pickle looked at the little girl, willing her to pick up the tights and try again. He was sure she could do it. He would give anything to have arms just to be able to help her.

The little girl got up and opened a cupboard and pulled out a round ball type thing. She squeezed it over and over in her hands.

Whatever the ball thing was, it seemed to calm her down a bit.

After what seemed like an eternity, the little girl reached over for the tights and tried again. This time she succeeded and with that she put on the rest of her uniform without issue, scooped him up, and bounced down the stairs for breakfast.

Before long, they were in the car again, but just the daddy this time. He wondered if the mummy was too sad to come with them, or maybe she had to stay and look after whoever this Pumpkin character was!

The little girl was singing along to the songs at the top of her voice. *She has such a lovely voice*, Pickle thought, and he closed his eyes and listened contentedly.

It wasn't long before the car stopped and the daddy got out, but the little girl seemed to stay put. The daddy opened her door and reached in for her book bag and lunchbox.

Pickle suddenly felt very hot and he realised the little girl was holding him too tight again.

What was wrong with the little girl? he thought.

Without any warning she kicked the back of the seat, which confused Pickle as no one was sitting in it this time.

"Let's go, darling," the daddy said.

The little girl stayed seated.

The heavy tension seemed to surround them again until eventually the little girl reluctantly left the car and grabbed the daddy's hand. Pickle was relieved as she then slowly released her grip on him.

Pickle looked around him as he was being carried.

Wow, it was so busy! There were people everywhere, and children running, shouting, and screaming.

Cars were zooming up and down the road; even an ambulance whizzed by, sirens going and lights flashing.

He glanced up at the little girl again — he could tell she was struggling.

They stopped walking and stood still near the entrance.

Pickle wondered if this was where they said goodbye to the daddy.

Most of the children had already gone in and the playground suddenly seemed eerily quiet.

The daddy bent down to the little girl and kissed the top of her head as if to say goodbye and started to turn around.

To Pickle's surprise, the little girl grabbed the daddy tightly, threw her book bag down and growled.

"Come on," the daddy said. "Mrs Dover is here now and she will take you in."

The little girl clung onto the daddy tighter and tried to push Mrs Dover away.

The teacher attempted to edge closer, but the little girl hissed and snarled at her.

Another teacher joined them. He was very tall and looked a bit frightening.

Pickle looked up at the little girl again, but she had somehow managed to escape from everyone and run off in the opposite direction, leaving Pickle upside down in the daddy's hand, which, thankfully, was not at all sweaty.

"Listen, you head off and we will sort it out," Mrs Dover said.

The daddy sighed heavily and handed Pickle over to her. "Please give her this when you can."

Mrs Dover placed Pickle in her palm. "Of course," she said, looking faintly surprised.

Pickle met her gaze. *Didn't she know how important he was to the little girl?* he thought.

The daddy turned around and strode back to the car. Pickle wondered how he was feeling. Did this happen every day when they arrived at school?

Maybe the little girl had run back to the car. If she had, maybe they could all return to the safety of home. He didn't like this school place one bit and he hadn't even been inside yet!

Mrs Dover made her way back into the school building, carefully carrying Pickle.

He looked behind them and spotted the frightening man walking back with the little girl.

She didn't look very happy, but at least she was walking in the right direction, he thought.

As they got closer, the little girl immediately asked, "Where's Pickle?"

"Is this him?" Mrs Dover asked, handing him over.

The little girl nodded and popped him in her pocket.

Pickle sighed. The day had barely begun and he was totally exhausted. Whatever would happen next?

Pickle felt hot. He wished he could climb out of the little girl's pocket.

Then, as if by magic, he was lifted out and placed on a wooden desk. He sighed with relief. It was as if the little girl had read his mind!

He looked around. There were little girls and boys everywhere and the noise — oh my, the noise — it was deafening!

He looked up at the little girl and was surprised to see that she had her hands covering her ears.

Suddenly, she jumped off her chair and crawled under her desk.

Is this a new game? Pickle thought. He hoped so — it looked kind of fun!

He looked around him to see what the other little children were doing. They were all still talking loudly. *How odd*, he thought. *Maybe they weren't in the mood to play?*

"Quiet everyone," boomed a voice at the front.

Pickle recognised the man — he was the frightening one from earlier that chased after the little girl. *Hmmm, this could be interesting*, he thought.

The room fell silent, but the little girl stayed under the desk. Pickle wondered if the teacher would notice. He hoped she wouldn't get told off.

Time ticked by, and although the teacher was still talking, Pickle had switched off, concerned only for the little girl.

He wondered if she had these butterflies in her tummy that she had warned him about. She was awfully quiet under there.

He also wondered if any of the butterflies would fly out. Would the other children try and catch them? He hoped not. They belonged to the little girl!

Suddenly, the desk jolted, he was swooped up swiftly and the little girl ran out of the classroom.

He felt sick. He was feeling sick a lot lately!

A door slammed shut and the little girl sat down on something. He looked around. They seemed to be in some sort of cubicle. It was small and smelt a bit funny.

The little girl had tears running down her face and was sobbing.

"I need help," she whispered. "This is your time to help me fight off the others."

Others, he thought. *Where?* He glanced around nervously and wished he was equipped with some sort of sword.

"I can't cope, Pickle," she confided. "There's too much noise, too many children."

She stroked him harder as she spoke, clearly upset.

Just then he heard a door open. Footsteps clicked along the floor until they stopped outside of their cubicle.

The little girl seemed to stop breathing for a minute, but her tears were still silently running down her red, puffy cheeks.

"Are you okay in there?" a lady asked.

The little girl shook her head, but made no noise. Oh, how Pickle wished he could talk for her.

"I'm just here if you need me," she said.

The little girl let out a breath.

What were they going to do now? he wondered. The smell was getting a bit overpowering for him.

"We could go to my office and play with some Lego. Or make some slime, if you like."

The little girl sat up straight, suddenly interested.

"In your own time, though. I'll just be out here."

The little girl wiped her eyes with the sleeve of her jumper and slowly opened the cubicle door.

Mrs Dover was standing there, a concerned look on her face.

She held out her hand and the little girl reluctantly took hold and they all walked down to her office.

Once inside, the little girl sat at the table with a box of Lego. *She looks much happier,* Pickle thought as she started sorting the Lego into colours and shapes.

Suddenly, a loud bell rang and the little girl jumped off her seat and cowered in the corner, leaving him perched up high on some Lego construction.

What on earth was going on now? he thought.

"It's break time," Mrs Dover said.

The little girl hissed, just like a snake again. She seemed to be doing a lot of that lately. It worried Pickle as he didn't think she was doing it for fun.

He glanced up at Mrs Dover who didn't look quite so friendly now.

The office door swung open and two more teachers walked in — one was the frightening man from earlier. *What did he want now?* Pickle thought.

"Come on, then. Time to get some fresh air," and the frightening man edged closer to the little girl.

She kicked out, hard. Boy did she look angry. The other teacher came forward and she got the same treatment, too, and narrowly missed a bit of random Lego aimed at her head.

They backed away, whispering to each other.

On the way out, the frightening man spotted Pickle sat on top of the lego masterpiece and picked him up.

The little girl growled and Pickle suddenly feared for his life! Were they going to throw him away? He closed his eyes tight.

Next thing he knew, he was passed down to the little girl, who grabbed him like her life depended on it.

Pickle looked around him. The room was empty now. Where had everyone gone?

But then he spotted the frightening man just outside, peering in at them around the corner.

The little girl didn't seem to notice and he thought that was probably for the best as she didn't seem to like people crowding her.

After a while, the little girl got up, brushed down her skirt and slowly edged out of the office.

Pickle hoped the man would move out of the way in time. If she spotted him, Pickle felt sure there could be more problems.

They reached the door. The corridor was quiet, thankfully, and the little girl slowly walked away like nothing had happened.

When the time came, lunch seemed to go without a hitch, but he did find it strange that the little girl didn't eat with all the other school children. She ate her lunch in an office with another little boy. They seemed friends as they were talking lots.

Pickle didn't understand much about the conversation, but a word he heard over and over was Minecraft. He wondered if that was a lesson at school. If so, he thought the little girl wouldn't be under the desk then as she seemed so animated talking about it!

She appeared to enjoy the next lesson, too. Well, she wasn't hiding, so Pickle thought that must be a good thing.

He looked at her shyly again. Her eyes were bright, all signs of tears and anger gone. Pickle noticed that the sun coming in from the window cast a soft glow on top of the little girl's head, making her blonde hair shine. *Almost like a halo*, he thought.

She really was rather pretty and Pickle wondered if he was starting to be a tiny bit in love with her.

He snapped himself back to reality just as quickly and tried to concentrate on the lesson.

The little girl was busily writing something down, but Pickle couldn't make sense of it. There seemed to be numbers all across the page, some in columns and some just dotted around.

The teacher was walking up and down and stopped next to the little girl. Pickle held his breath.

The teacher bent over, looked at the page and said, "Well done. You've got them all right."

The little girl smiled, but seemed a bit embarrassed, too.

It was funny, Pickle thought. *The little girl seemed happy in this class, but there was still the same number of children.*

The class was a bit quieter he supposed, but not much. The little girl did seem to enjoy working these numbers out, so perhaps that was the key — if she was doing something she enjoyed, she could block everything and everyone else out and the butterflies in her tummy would disappear.

He thought back to one of his first conversations with the little girl where she tried to explain about Autism and something else. What was it now?... PPA?

He really couldn't remember and hoped she would open up about that again. He felt he would need to know a whole lot more about it to understand and help her better.

The Bath

Pickle must have fallen asleep, for when he awoke they were no longer in the school, but instead he was back on the windowsill in the little girl's bedroom.

The little girl was bouncing on a big blue ball.

"Bath's ready!" the mummy called out.

The little girl didn't answer. A few minutes ticked by, but she continued to bounce. The TV was switched off and she seemed to be lost in a little world all of her own.

Pickle wondered if now that he was part of the family, would he be expected to have a bath, too? He hoped so! He loved being in the water.

"I've switched on the fairy lights for you," the mummy called out again.

The little girl ignored her and continued to bounce.

The mummy suddenly appeared in the doorway. Pickle could tell she was beginning to get a little agitated.

"Come on, before the water gets cold," she said.

The little girl ignored her.

"Well, I will leave you to it. You could always take Pickle in with you. He's become a bit grubby lately, too." She smiled at him.

Hey! thought Pickle, *That's not funny.* And there he was thinking the mummy was a nice mummy. Maybe he thought wrong!

The little girl stopped bouncing.

Aha, thought Pickle. *Maybe she was ready now.*

The mummy went back downstairs and the little girl turned to Pickle. "You are rather dirty," she exclaimed with a twinkle in her eye.

Hey, thought Pickle, *you are meant to be my friend. I was going to fight battles for you!*

She took him into the bathroom where the fairy lights cast a sort of magical glow, making the water appear even more inviting.

Pickle averted his eyes as the little girl stripped off and jumped in the bath, causing a big splash. She dunked Pickle in the water before finally balancing him on a sponge.

"You okay, Pumpkin?" the mummy called up.

Oh no, thought Pickle, *not that Pumpkin again*. He hoped he wouldn't have to share a bath with him, too. There really wasn't enough room!

"Yes," the little girl said and continued to flick water at Pickle.

After some time the mummy appeared again. "Ready to do hair?" she asked.

"Can we do it tomorrow instead?" the little girl protested.

"Well, as you are in the bath now, it makes sense to get it done," the mummy said in a no-nonsense tone.

The little girl didn't look too happy at this suggestion. Pickle wondered what would happen now, for there was certainly no desk to climb under this time, no shoes to throw, and no car seat to kick. He held his breath.

It seemed the little girl really didn't like to be told what to do and when to do it!

The mummy reached up for the shower hose and turned the water on again.

Pickle hadn't seen anyone have their hair washed before.

"Ow, you are burning my head!" the little girl shouted.

"Don't be silly," the mummy said and continued.

"I can't see!" the little girl screamed next.

Pickle panicked — could water on your head make you go blind?

The mummy passed a towel to the little girl and sighed heavily.

"My head's on fire!" the little girl screamed.

Fire?! Pickle thought. *Quick! Someone better ring the fire brigade! Why was the mummy not rushing to the phone? Didn't she care what happened to the little girl?*

Pickle took a quick look at the little girl. On closer inspection, there didn't appear to be flames on her head. Phew! Emergency over.

"We're nearly done," the mummy said. "Just a bit of conditioner and that's it."

Thankfully, the little girl remained quiet until the water was finally turned off.

Stepping out of the bath, the mummy wrapped the little girl in a big fluffy towel. Whatever had just happened between them was thankfully short-lived and peace was restored.

The mummy stood up, about to leave, but the little girl pulled her closer. "Can we just cuddle for a bit, like this?" she asked sleepily, reaching out with open arms.

"Of course, Pumpkin," the mummy said softly

Here we go again, thought Pickle. This Pumpkin guy better show himself soon — he wanted to have words with him!

Pickle studied the little girl and the mummy. They really did look very much alike.

The mummy sniffed and when Pickle looked at her again, he noticed her eyes were watery, just like the other day. Pickle frowned. *Why would the mummy be upset? Didn't she like cuddles?*

Humans were hard to understand.

Pickle closed his eyes and prayed bathtime was not going to be every night. He didn't think he could cope with fires, burning heads, and the little girl going blind again. What a day!

Friendships

"It's the weekend, Pickle. You know what that means, don't you?" the little girl exclaimed, grinning from ear to ear.

"No school!" she said and jumped up and down in excitement.

She then switched on the TV and settled down in her special chair. "Today is going to be all about Minecraft," she said.

Pickle tried to remember where he had heard that word before.

The little girl put him down on the carpet and placed a funny controller thing in front of him. "This one is yours," she said. "We can play together."

Pickle wondered how this was going to work, given he was just a pebble, but he went along with it anyway.

"Yay! My friends are online," she exclaimed, picking up the controller and starting to furiously stab at the buttons.

The little girl then put on her headphones and proceeded to talk animatedly. He wondered who she was talking to, but she never did say. Maybe it was the elusive Pumpkin character?

Pickle soon switched off. After all, he couldn't really join in, could he? Once again he found himself wishing he had arms, fingers, and thumbs.

He must have dozed off, for when he woke up the little girl was no longer slouched in her gaming chair — she was bouncing on the big blue ball again, still holding the controller.

Pickle noticed her hands had turned a little red where she was gripping it very tightly.

She was shouting something at the screen, but Pickle couldn't really make out what she was saying as the words made no sense to him.

Within seconds she ripped the headphones off and threw them at the window, knocking her globe off the windowsill.

Oh no, not again, Pickle thought. He looked around for cover.

"You okay?" the daddy shouted up the stairs.

The little girl ignored him. She seemed to do a lot of that, Pickle noticed. Or maybe she was going deaf. After all, she went blind the other day in the bath!

"No!" she shouted back.

Aha, so she did hear, thought Pickle. Maybe she just took longer to process the question for some reason. Pickle frowned and wondered if that had anything to do with the PPA or whatever it was called.

The daddy came up the stairs and started talking to the little girl, and although Pickle tried to follow the conversation, the little girl was talking too quickly. The daddy seemed to understand though, thankfully.

"Why didn't you tell them how you felt?" the daddy asked.

The little girl remained quiet, her head bowed.

Pickle looked at the TV and made out some sort of forest, but a building in the middle sort of looked trashed. He didn't really understand.

"They came onto my world and destroyed everything!" the little girl sobbed. "Why would they do that?"

"Oh, darling," the daddy said and swooped the little girl up for a cuddle.

Eventually the sobbing subsided.

From what Pickle could make out, it seems she was playing with these 'so-called' friends when one of them turned on her and started to destroy the world she was trying to build for them all.

When the daddy asked her why she didn't tell them to stop, the little girl said because otherwise they wouldn't want to play with her again. Pickle was pretty sure this wasn't how friendships worked. Surely your friends couldn't mess up something you were doing without any consequences?

"Darling, Gemma's here and she wants to know if you want to come out and play?" the mummy shouted up the stairs.

The daddy looked at the little girl. "Do you?" he asked, concern in his voice.

The little girl wiped her eyes, nodded, and picked up Pickle.

On the way out of the bedroom, Pickle caught a glance of the daddy resting his head in his hands. *Maybe he was tired, too,* Pickle thought. Things were certainly hectic in this house!

Pickle was soon introduced to Gemma, whom he liked immediately and decided was worthy of his friendship. Unlike the little boy who had laughed at him the other day, this little girl thought his name was 'well cool' and she even gave him a little kiss.

Steady on, thought Pickle, for he was already taken!

"Shall we get our skates?" Gemma asked.

"Great idea!" the little girl replied.

Soon, Pickle was having a whale of a time, zooming up and down the road. And he never felt sick once. Bonus!

After a short while, some other children came out of their houses nearby. They all joined together, talking loudly to each other and laughing at something someone said.

Suddenly, Pickle felt the little girl's hand clasp him harder. He was unsure why, as he thought they were all her friends and were having fun. Maybe like at school, it was all getting a bit too noisy for the little girl.

Someone pushed the little girl, and he felt her squeeze him tighter, if that was at all possible.

Pickle looked round to see who it was. It was that silly boy again, from the other day.

"Where's your stone friend now?" he shouted out.

The little girl stayed quiet.

"Leave her alone," Gemma said, putting her arm around her friend.

The little boy leaned right into the little girl's face and said, "Give me your stone."

The little girl stepped back and said, "It's not a stone, for a start. It's a pebble."

This seemed to confuse the little boy, who once again, tried to push the little girl.

"Give it to me," he demanded.

And with that, the little girl turned on her heel and ran back into the safety of the house, slamming the door shut behind her.

Gemma stared after her, disappointed that she no longer had her friend to play with.

She considered going to knock again for her, but then thought better of it.

She felt sad, for although she didn't always understand her friend, she knew she reacted to things differently, and she — like Pickle — only wanted to help her.

Perhaps they could play again tomorrow, minus the silly boy, of course!

Meds

It was warm in the house compared to being outside. The mummy and daddy were sitting at the kitchen table drinking coffee when the little girl burst in through the door and made her way straight to the fridge.

"You okay?" they asked in unison.

The little girl didn't reply but plonked Pickle on the table, grabbed something to eat and went to go upstairs.

"Hey, hang on a minute," the daddy said. "It's time to do meds."

"I'll do them later," the little girl said and made for the stairs again.

"What about Pickle?" the mummy asked, picking him up. "He wants to see you take them."

Pickle frowned. He didn't remember saying that.

The little girl stopped in her tracks, turned around and looked over at Pickle.

The room seemed to fill with tension, just like when they were waiting in the car for the dentist.

"I'll just get them ready," the daddy said and stood up.

The mummy handed Pickle to the little girl. "Here you are," she said.

The little girl took him and paced up and down the kitchen floor, back and forth. Before he knew it, he was placed on the table again and the little girl started jumping over the kitchen chair, and then on and off the sofa.

Why on earth was she doing that? Pickle wondered. *Was this another strange game he would need to learn?*

He looked over at the mummy, but she seemed to be ignoring it, so Pickle decided to ignore it, too.

"There you go," the daddy said and handed the little girl a glass with a small amount of liquid in it.

The little girl banged the glass down on the table and continued pacing up and down, jumping over the chair again and again. Her face was getting redder, Pickle noticed.

Pickle suddenly spotted the little black dog sitting in his basket. He seemed to be shivering. *That's odd*, Pickle thought, *for he hadn't been outside in the cold.*

"Right," said the daddy and handed the little girl the glass for the second time. Pickle supposed she was meant to drink it.

The mummy looked up and locked eyes with the daddy.

"Five…" said the little girl suddenly.

"Four…" said the daddy.

"Three…" said the mummy.

This must be part of the game Pickle thought.

"Two…" said the little girl.

Then they all looked at Pickle expectantly. He tried so hard to speak and say "one" but nothing came out.

For a split second the little girl looked disappointed and Pickle felt sad. He wished he had a mouth and could talk.

They all shouted out, "One!" and the little girl downed the medicine and banged the glass on the table with a thud.

"Done!" she said.

The next minute, the little girl was looking in the fridge again, clearly hungry.

"Well done," the mummy and daddy said.

The little girl smiled and looked much happier. She grabbed a handful of grapes and said, "Come on, Pickle, let's go upstairs."

He desperately wanted to ask her what the medicine was for, but thankfully she beat him to it.

"I actually don't mind taking the medicine. It just depends what mood I'm in," she said. "But don't tell that to Mummy and Daddy!"

Pickle frowned, wondering why she created such a fuss about it then.

"It's just feels like such a demand to take it, and inside I feel I have to do all I can to not take it. If that makes sense, Pickle."

Pickle wasn't sure he understood.

"The medicine helps to calm me down," she said. "I never thought it used to help, but I know now that it actually does."

"It also helps me focus much better and I don't get as angry as I used to."

Pickle thought she had become pretty angry earlier, so life before taking medicine must have been really bad.

He had so many questions to ask, but knew he had to remain patient until the little girl opened up some more.

"I've done some not very nice things in the past," she said sadly. "I don't remember everything, but I know it wasn't good."

She picked Pickle up and held him on her lap, stroking him gently.

"Mummy and Daddy are trying to find me a different school. They don't understand me, where I go now," she said. "They just end up making everything worse."

The little girl sighed. She seemed to have the weight of the world on her young shoulders. "I sometimes wish I didn't have PDA."

Ahh yes, that was it. PDA, not PPA, Pickle thought.

The little girl continued, "PDA is part of the autism spectrum, but many people, even some professionals, don't think it's real. But it is, Pickle. How can they even think it's not?"

Pickle was confused now.

"PDA is closely linked to anxiety," she said. "When someone tells me to do something, sometimes I actually can't do it. It's not because I am naughty though, Pickle, or I don't want to. It's because I physically can't at that particular moment. I need to be in control and do things the way I want to do them," she continued.

Pickle thought this could be very difficult to achieve, especially in school where you are always being told what to do and when to do it.

"Sometimes I think teachers are a threat, even if they are just trying to talk to me. I know it sounds silly, Pickle, but I really struggle. In fact, sometimes I even make out I am okay and happy when I'm not. There's a word for that — do you know what it is?" she asked.

Pickle tried to shake his head but couldn't. He was getting mighty fed up just being a pebble.

"It's called masking," the little girl explained. "It means I pretend everything is okay and that I am coping, when in reality I just want to hide in the loo, like you and I did, remember?"

Pickle tried to nod but couldn't do that either. *Agggghhhh!* he thought.

"Trouble is, Pickle, I can only mask for a short time. Otherwise, the 'other pebbles' build up in my tummy and I explode, usually when I get home as that is where I feel most safe. Then poor Mummy and Daddy have to try and calm me down. I know it can't be easy for them. The sad thing is, Pickle, I think I might have hurt them, too, but I don't really remember." The little girl hung her head, deep in thought.

Pickle turned his thoughts to the mummy and daddy sat downstairs and he felt a bit sad, wondering how hard it was to try and calm the little girl down, for she seemed ready to explode so often.

"That's why I have you to help me," the little girl said and held him up to her face.

Christmas

"I'm so excited, Pickle!" the little girl said when they were on her bed relaxing together one day.

"It's soon going to be Christmas!" she squealed with delight.

Christmas? Pickle thought. He had no idea what it was, but the little girl certainly sounded excited.

"I can't wait to put the tree up and decorate it with all the pretty lights. And we must remember to leave out a drink and some cookies for Santa, and carrots for his reindeer."

Pickle had no idea what she was talking about, but she seemed happy and that rubbed off on him, too.

The little girl suddenly looked sad. "Last year was awful, Pickle," she said. "We didn't know then about my diagnosis and we had the worst Christmas ever. Mummy and Daddy didn't really understand me as much then either."

Pickle wondered what on earth had happened, and how did having a diagnosis — whatever that was — make such a big difference?

"I got so overwhelmed on the day — there were so many presents, too much noise and way too many people here in the house. I wish I'd had you back then. You would have been able to help me."

Pickle wasn't sure how, but was pleased to think she thought he could have helped her.

"This year, Mummy and Daddy said it's going to be totally different, and I will be able to have some of my presents early if I want to. Well, I obviously will, won't I, Pickle? Let's face it, who wouldn't?" she enthused.

"I don't even have to have the dinner Daddy cooks, either. I can eat whatever I want!" she proudly proclaimed. "I can stuff my face silly all day long," and she laughed.

Pickle noticed a theme here: the little girl seemed to love her food and seemed to be constantly hungry!

"We aren't having anyone over, either. Well, not on Christmas day, anyway," she said. "It will just be us five."

Five? Pickle thought. He ran through the family members in his mind: the little girl, himself, the mummy and daddy… but that was four.

Suddenly, it dawned on him. The little black dog — he must be the fifth member of the family. He supposed it was only fair that the dog was allowed to join in the celebrations, too.

A few days later, the tree was up, lights twinkled wherever you looked, and there seemed to be a different feel in the air — no tension at all, just a magical sort of excitement.

Pickle thought a lot of it was to do with the fact that school had finished and the little girl seemed to spend most of her days either playing in her room with the controller thing or taking the little black dog for a walk with her parents at the local park. She seemed to be taking her medicine better, too, which in turn made the mummy and daddy happier as well. Life seemed pretty good.

"I hope we get snow, Pickle," the little girl said. "You would love it!"

Pickle wished he knew what snow meant.

"Mummy loves Christmas. She always tells me about what it was like when she was a little girl growing up and how magical it was. I love hearing her stories, Pickle. They make me feel all warm and fuzzy inside."

Later, when they were all sitting in the lounge, Christmas music playing in the background, the little black dog bounded in and jumped up on the daddy's lap. The little girl jumped on the daddy, too, and soon all of them were play wrestling on the floor.

Pickle wished he could join in — it looked so much fun! — but he stayed close to the mummy, just in case the dog licked him to death. He didn't want to die and not experience Christmas!

The little girl screamed and for a moment Pickle thought she had hurt herself, but the mummy laughed, and he realised they were still playing and the daddy was tickling her, which she seemed to love.

It was so lovely to hear the little girl laugh out loud, and he wished he could hear more of her laughter, as that made him feel all warm and fuzzy inside, too, just like the little girl had explained earlier.

The tickling soon stopped and the little girl got to her feet. "I'm starving!" she pronounced, and everyone laughed again, even the little black dog!

This was going to be the best Christmas ever!

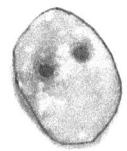

Christmas was indeed a magical time for the whole family.

Days seemed to roll into one another and although there wasn't snow like the little girl hoped, there was still plenty of fun in the house. Everyone's mood seemed lighter, too. There didn't seem to be any expectations or rules to follow, Pickle noticed. The little girl didn't even clean her teeth one night, but no one commented on it.

He remembered the little girl telling him how she used to struggle with brushing her teeth when younger and how the mummy and daddy decided she needed two different coloured toothbrushes so she could choose which one to use. It seems offering the little girl a choice made her much happier. Now, the little girl had a posh electric toothbrush. She showed him it one day and let him feel the sensation of the bristles. It was the most ticklyist thing he had ever felt, but the little girl absolutely loved using it.

When listening to her talk, it seemed to Pickle that the little girl had had many things to overcome throughout her life so far.

But the thing that made him the most sad was hearing about this masking she had to do at school. He remembered how suffocated he had felt in her pocket, and that was only for a short time. Masking all day must be unbearable.

December rolled into January and the start of a fresh new year. Pickle spent his days going to the school with the little girl. Some days were good, others not so good. The teachers never seemed to totally understand her, but he was learning so much about how she dealt with all the obstacles in her life.

The mummy and daddy got called into the school sometimes. Pickle wasn't sure why, but they never looked particularly happy about it. On some days at school, the little girl wouldn't talk at all, not even to him. He knew it wasn't anything he had done to upset her, but it still made him sad, especially when the other children at school made fun of her.

The little girl often spoke of the 'other pebbles' and sometimes he felt a bit worried. Were these other pebbles bigger than him? The little girl still hadn't given him anything to fight with. Surely she should have given him a weapon or something! He thought back to the time the little girl had told the daddy that she had ten pebbles. That was a lot of pebbles to contend with and fight off!

Great News

"We've got some great news!" the mummy said early one morning.

The little girl was barely awake. She rubbed her eyes and sat up.

"You know that school that Daddy and I looked around a while ago? Well, they have a space for you now! Isn't that amazing?"

The little girl was wide awake now. This was big news indeed!

She picked up Pickle and rolled him over in her hand. "Will I be able to take Pickle each day?"

The mummy laughed. "Of course," she said.

The little girl jumped up excitedly. "Can we look at the school again on the internet?" she asked.

The mummy took her phone out of her pocket and the three of them studied the website.

The daddy appeared in the doorway. "Who wants pancakes for breakfast?"

"Me, please!" everyone answered, except Pickle. Just because he couldn't talk he was going to miss out. That didn't seem fair to him!

"Don't forget one for Pickle," the little girl said.

Phew! thought Pickle. He was falling more in love with this little girl by the minute!

At the breakfast table, the little girl sat eating her pancakes, lost in thought.

"When do I start?" she asked.

"In two weeks," the daddy replied. "Mummy and I can't believe it. This school is going to be amazing for you, darling."

The little girl grinned. "Tell me again what the head teacher told you when you visited," she asked.

"Well," the daddy began, "it's a very small school, only about eight children to a class. You don't have to wear a uniform, and you can even call the teachers by their first names!"

The little girl's eyes widened. "So I won't wear a uniform, like I do now?"

"That's right," the mummy said. "You can wear whatever you want to wear... within reason, of course," and she smiled.

"Wow," the little girl said as she carried on munching for a bit.

"Do you think the teachers will be nicer and more understanding?" she asked, suddenly concerned.

Pickle was pretty sure they would. Otherwise, what would be the point of moving schools?

"Most definitely," the mummy and daddy answered together.

The little girl smiled and her whole face lit up. Pickle felt a warm glow, for he too, was looking forward to this new school.

Maybe everything was going to be much better from now on. He couldn't cross his fingers as…well…he didn't have any, so he crossed his eyes instead!

"It's okay to feel nervous. It's your first day," the daddy said.

The little girl was standing in the middle of her room, dressed in leggings and an old t-shirt.

"It just feels funny wearing this," she said, pulling at her top.

"It's fine," the daddy said. "Remember, we said that a lot of learning will be outside, so what you are wearing is fine."

"I suppose," she replied.

"And don't forget, you will be able to see the horses there, too!"

"Oh, yes!" she exclaimed. That was one of the great things about the school — the fact there were horses there that you could actually ride was just amazing!

She had always loved horses and now she could see them every single day. Some of her friends would be sooo jealous!

They pulled up outside the school. The little girl took a deep breath. She had seen pictures of the school, but it looked a bit different in real life.

"Are you and Pickle ready?" the daddy asked.

Pickle was secretly hoping she wasn't about to kick the back of the seat or anything. He held his breath.

The mummy got out and opened the car door.

The little girl jumped out, holding Pickle tight.

A young teacher walked towards them, smiling.

"Good morning," she said. "I'm Beth."

The little girl didn't meet her gaze, but held onto the daddy, scuffing her shoe on the gravel.

Oh no, thought Pickle, remembering the old school and what used to happen there.

"Shall we go and see the horses first?" Beth asked.

Yes! thought Pickle. That was the way to do it.

The little girl hesitated ever so slightly, then kissed the mummy and daddy goodbye and walked off holding Beth's hand. She didn't even look back!

Pickle did, however, and he saw the mummy and daddy cuddling. The mummy looked a bit upset — he wasn't sure why, as surely they would be happy. Why were humans so complicated?

Pickle watched them drive off down the road and prayed the little girl would have a good day.

"So, how was your first day?" the mummy and daddy asked excitedly when they arrived to collect the little girl.

Pickle had so much he wanted to say, but, of course, he couldn't. He hoped the little girl would open up, for she had had an amazing day. He willed her to tell them everything, and she did, thankfully!

On arriving home the little girl even asked for a bath. This was unheard of, apparently, but Pickle wasn't surprised as they both had got a bit grubby today feeding the horses. Well, he hadn't actually fed them himself, obviously, but he did get to have a little ride on one. Never again — he had felt so ill! He would leave the horse riding to the little girl in the future.

They had climbed trees and built camps. The little girl had loved that and told the teacher she wanted to do it every day. Pickle was pretty certain she would be able to — this school seemed to understand the little girl so much better already.

New Start

The first week went by without a hitch. Pickle noticed how happy the little girl was each morning, and how much more chatty she was to everyone.

Pickle was actually quite thankful he couldn't talk, as he wouldn't have been able to get a word in edgeways anyway!

The mummy and daddy seemed much happier, too. Even the little black dog hadn't been shaking for ages.

One night, he overheard the mummy and daddy talking downstairs. They were talking about the little girl and how tired she was in the evenings.

They weren't wrong, for she was falling asleep way before Pickle, which was most unusual. She wasn't playing much on the TV thing either. He supposed the fresh air was making her more sleepy.

He also noticed how she hadn't said a bad word about any of the teachers... so far. They were obviously doing something right. Maybe they understood PDA. He really hoped this school was going to work out for the little girl. She deserved that much.

She hadn't even had to mask, either, and had told him so the other evening.

"I can just be me," she said. "No-one judges me, and if I do something weird like this" and she made a strange dolphin sound in the back of her throat, "no one takes a blind bit of notice! It's great!"

Pickle remembered hearing that noise before. If he was honest, he wasn't so keen on it, and he hoped she wouldn't do it too near the horses in case she scared them off!

The second week was just as good, and the little girl slowly began to make friends. Pickle noticed though, that one little girl always seemed to be alone, especially at play times. He wondered if she, too, had pebbles. Maybe he would be called upon to fight them off for her as well?

"What's your name?" the little girl asked the lonely little girl one lunchtime.

"Layla," she replied.

"Do you want to come and play with me?" the little girl asked.

"Or we could go and stroke the horses if you prefer?"

Layla seemed to perk up and nodded meekly.

They all made their way over to the field, which was extremely muddy. Pickle hoped the little girl wouldn't drop him — he really didn't want to get too dirty!

The little girl tried to make conversation with Layla, but she didn't talk much. Pickle understood, though. In fact, he understood quite a bit more than people gave him credit for.

"Oh look," the little girl exclaimed, picking something up from ground.

It was a small pebble, quite shiny-looking, considering how much mud it had on it.

The little girl passed it over for Layla to hold.

"I've got a story to tell you, Layla. Keep hold of this pebble and I'll begin."

Layla nodded.

The girls took off their coats and found a dry patch in the field. The horses had wandered off for their feed. The sky was bluer than blue, the birds were singing, and it was incredibly peaceful.

Pickle noticed the peace, too. No teachers invading their space, no cars zooming by, no noisy children... just peace and nature all around them.

The little girl took Pickle out of her pocket, settled him on her lap, and began to tell Layla all about their adventures so far.

Layla listened intently, instantly hooked.

At the end of the story, the little girl placed Pickle in Layla's hand, next to the new pebble.

"These two are going to be best friends, I can just feel it. Just like us."

The two girls looked at each other and smiled shyly.

The little girl took Pickle back and popped him back on her lap, grinning. "You need to think of a name for yours, though. He can't start to help you until you name him," she said, looking serious.

Layla paused, as if in deep thought, and looked up. "I shall name him Pumpkin!" she said excitedly. Pickle couldn't believe it — what was this fascination with pumpkins?!

"My mum calls me that sometimes," the little girl said.

"No way! Mine, too!" Layla said.

Both girls laughed and hugged, sensing they had much more in common than they first realised.

"So, tell me again — where did you actually find Pickle?" Layla asked.

"On the beach at Durdle Door. I just knew he was the one," she said. "And as soon as I saw Pumpkin, I knew he would be the one for you, too."

Layla grinned.

"Come on Layla, let's go and introduce Beth to our new best friends!"

The girls raced back to the school. Pickle glanced over at Pumpkin in Layla's hand and smiled.

Let the 'Team Pebble' adventures begin!

About the Author

Zelda Mothins is the mother of a complex little girl diagnosed in 2019 with ADHD and autism with Pathological Demand Avoidance (PDA).

After a turbulent mainstream school life, Zelda's daughter now attends a specialist setting where she is finally flourishing.

By witnessing the extreme highs and lows of her daughter's navigation through life along with ever-changing emotions and need for control, Zelda was inspired to bring the family's experiences to life through *The Adventures of Pickle*.

Beautifully illustrated throughout, let Pickle take you on a very special journey.

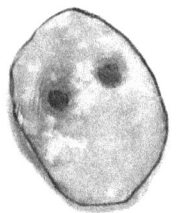

www.ingramcontent.com/pod-product-compliance
Lightning Source LLC
Chambersburg PA
CBHW041148110526

44590CB00027B/4164